The Tide of Life

By Christopher A Geary

The Tide of Life

Christopher A Geary

Copyright © 2021 Christopher A Geary

ISBN:9798568366966

First Edition

Instagram-Gearysworld
Facebook page- Gearysworld-Art by
Christopher Geary
Twitter-GearyArt

Contents

3

Foreword

First of all, thank you for purchasing this book. This is the first collection of my poems. I picked the title "The Tide of Life" because it covers a large spectrum of subjects. The poems I have been writing on and off for around five years. They come from observations, experiences and conversations I have had.

The poems are designed to make you think, conjure up images, make you laugh and many other feelings. I hope you enjoy them; some tell stories, some make statements.

The ideas have been inspired by friends, and things around me. They have been collected from social media status updates, notes in journals and on scraps of paper to hopefully form a coherent narrative.

I am hoping you will take something away from this book. These are my thoughts I am sharing; that in itself is a little scary. I am really hoping it will invoke images of great imagination.

I hope you enjoy this collection of poems grabbed from many places to form this book. It's been great putting it together.

I would consider myself an amateur writer, but if you take something away from it that is fantastic and humbling at the same time.

Christopher A Geary 2021

The Tide of Life

The tide leaves things behind
Will it ever be kind?

Lots and lots stay together for a
while
Finding their own style.

Some will work
Some will rest
Some will even make a nest.

Best laid plans go back to sea
When it returns,
They will split and divide
Maybe even cast aside

It will return as before
Things new will be in store
All washed up on the shore.

Things that pave the way
Ready for another day
New and bright
Once again washed from sight

7.

Better Day

Don't know what
Don't know when
Can't say never again!

From now my future starts
Who knows if I lose or win?
But I will swim up against the tide
I may even gain some pride.

I shall begin to walk a path
Laugh along the way
Then will say, well, that was a
better day.

Shops Run by Little Ladies

Now when I was just ten in a
little Cotswold town
There were shops that were run
by little ladies.
All bright and very strict
They did rule this district.

The little paper shop
Was occupied by one with beady
eyes They watched you intently
With specs right down her nose
She stood on curled toes.

Then she would shout:
"This is not a library! If you're
not buying, which I doubt, could
you please get out!"
She would follow it with a glare
if you were in any doubt
She would stare until you were
out.

In the little grocery was a little
lady
Her face round like a blushing pie
"What can I do for you today?"
she would chuckle from beneath
her hair of purple dye.

On the crop of veggies sat a big
cat
No health and safety then to
cover your back.
He would play a game of dare
At you he would stare
His claws glistened in the dusty
Sunlight air.
Lots of the customers, well, they
just took flight until out of sight.

Then there was the shop that was
a tomb of old toys.
Piled to the ceiling boxes so old
Treasure hunting legends might
have been told
In the archive that never got sold.

This shopkeeper would appear if
by magic.
She looked you in the eye because
she wasn't very tall
She seemed to produce a large
boxed toy from out of sight.

You would marvel at the sale she
would entrap you in
"That will be sixpence" she said
with a grin
To refuse was, well a sin.

The sweet shop had a door like a
horse stable style.
On a table inside by the lower
door
Were jars of every type of sweet
you could imagine.

Sherbet saucers
Black jacks
Liquorice in strings
Round jellied rings
Stoppers for your gobs

Out her head would bob
Armed with a little shovel
A bag at the ready
She would fill very steady.
Taking orders by the dozen each
sweet would be measured
The sugary bags they would be
treasured.

Now all these shops are gone
Forty years on
The little ladies of which there
should be a song are sadly long
gone.

13

They Called Him...

They called him by a different
name
Too many had the same.

They called him to wash, clean the
floor
 Keep clear the fire door.

They called him to collect and
recycle things
He also emptied their rubbish bins.

They called him to despatch the
post
He did the dirtiest jobs
The jobs no one liked.
He did them without complaint
Now here they cannot remain.

Things will not be the same!
They called him out to say farewell
Things will work out they all said.

They called him to say we will all
be friends
He knows this to be true
There will be no end.

Good things will start to flourish
Our futures we will nourish
We will meet again
Things won't be the same!

They called him by a different
name
Now listen you had your game

Call me by my proper name.

Identity

I sometimes wonder
Where am I?
Who am I?
What is my path?
This I ponder!

Who am I to become?
Will I be better than before?
Will my future I adore?

Is it right, is it wrong?
Will I put it down on paper?
Will it be looked at as a bad caper?
What is my destiny to be?
Can you see?

Please tell me, what do you see?
See, I am confused!
With society I am bemused!
Work or play?
Do I have a say?

Do we ever know who we truly are?
I hope my guiding star will help me
flourish
Maybe with the results I will
nourish
With my own desire others I would
love to inspire
So myself I may find
I hope the journey may be kind.

The Sceptics

Oh no, that won't work
I hear them say.

You are wasting days on idle
dreams
You will fall apart at the seams

What a silly notion
You have to work
Put those dreams on the shelf
They will never work
Your duties you must not shirk.

Oh, I knew they could do it
I never doubted they all say
When they smell successes
Heaps and heaps of praise
When people you impress.

Follow your path
Don't be ruled by sceptics!
You can be that to yourself
So don't leave your dreams on the
shelf.

Make future the sceptics never
foresaw.
That will shut them up for sure.

Art Create

Each day I imagine a future of projects
I may shine that are truly mine
That's no whine.

Art Create
With word I start.
My chimes weird to some of futures
Telling stories
Not always for the glory.

It's a road hard to take
The gloating eyes I will shake.
They will see ideas laid straight
Some will like, some will hate
It may cause some debate.

So based on this mocked up status
You will either like or hate us
It's up to you how you rate us.
A poem writer and illustrator
I hope these words don't frustrate ya!

Hi-Vis

Hi-vis bin men recycle
Hi-vis warehouse packers, loading
Hi-vis builders constructing.

On diggers and on scaffold
They all work away
In their hi-vis to make a safer day

Hi-vis road workers
Dig never-ending holes
Laying out cones in long lines
Their time they seem to spend
Putting up signs, lights
They seem to start on red.

Hi-vis factory operatives make and
build
Their rank by hi-vis colour
Their authority it is sealed.

Red, orange, yellow, blue
Somewhere there is a hi-vis quite close
to you!

It's to make Mr Health and Safety
more aware
Hi-vis, hard hat, ear protectors, gloves
are needed
Yes, the rules you have succeeded!

Be safe in your hi-vis
The guidelines you must follow
Sometimes health and safety is a good
thing to do
Who knows, one day your hi-vis may
save you.

Flat Cap

Flat Cap chequered country green
Some old shoes that need repair.
He sits surveying his surround high
in his stool-type chair.
He may listen and pick up bits of
disjointed gossip
So he sits, his beer he does sip.

The young think they know it all
Have they learnt anything at all?
History repeats as time moves on
Same mistakes
Same vices
Some go far
Some stay put.

Not willing to listen to the old
It won't be long before they inherit
the old boy's seat
Then again repeat, repeat!

Granted technology and things will
change.
Nostalgia they will crave
Back to better days that weren't
It's just rose tinted in their
memories burnt.

Flap Cap watches as they tap
phones
This is where it's at
Do you have the latest app?

The young man sits with his mates
Time for some shots all round.

Young ladies come and wave and
titter, Some even order bitter
Then they all sit looking at their
phones
Not much talking then?

Flat Cap forgets when they did the
same
It's just newspapers they stuck
their faces in!
Back then you could tell the man
by what paper he would peruse
Now he did feel amused.

Then he is joined by more old hats
They reminisce about people and
things they do miss.
Another three ales please for me
John
and Jim
Hang on, you better get one for
him, late again
Chuckle! Chuckle!
You lot will get my knuckle!

The old and young drink and mix
together
They become a great local group
Mostly talk about the weather
Come rain or shine
Oi, that beer's mine.

22

23

Did you see the game?
That TV show?
Sorry I must go.

Then the night ends later than it
did in the day
Good night, see you soon.

So up the road they all go
Some in groups
Some alone.

Full of what the evening brought
It was a good night they all sought
Other nights they will enjoy.

Now late night diets they will
employ
Bacon sarnie?
Large kebab?
Fridge food that can be had?

Into bed they will stumble
In the morning they will tumble.

Flat Cap will wake early
Later down for another beer
More time and money he will
spend
Will the cycle never end?

A Dream Is

A dream is where you go to sleep
Good or bad, or sometimes sad
You may wake confused
Aroused or amused.

Frightened you may be
As you dream of things not nice
Of monsters that want to dice and
slice.

They may get stuck on repeat
So take a seat for the show
See where your dream may go.

If you dream in the light of day
About things you wish to do
Who knows it may come true.

So cloud nine you will follow
One joyful day say this is mine
On your happiness you will dine.

Your ship came in
You live the dream
Until the end of your time
Seize the dream, this is mine.

Others will aspire
From which you now retire
Their dream it will become
And what they most desire.

Bet You Don't Know What I Know!!

Hey, how are you?
Bet you don't know what I know!
Why, what do you know?
I heard something the other day!
Did you? What was that then?
You tell me what you know and I will
tell what I know!

Well I never!
Who would of thought that?
In their condition!
At their time of life!
Well now you know!

So it spreads like a fire
Chinese whispers
Idle gossip
From gate to gate it does spread.

Soon everyone knows what they know
With extra bits
More than when it started
It's not the same
They play a silly dangerous game.
Then the source says
Well I don't reckon all this can be true!

So if you know something
Be careful, it may not be true
It will come back to haunt you!

So what do you know then??

It's Here

The day has come
Is that three months gone already?
It's here, the time has come.

They are moving
Leaving us without work!
It did not last
Now it's left in the past.

The thing is we never shirked
We were quite busy
The victims of our own success
Now were put to duress.

The business wants to expand
It's too far for us to travel
So us they will dispend
This means we will unravel.

Not long ago they said
Things were fine
But now it's not, now
Things have changed and got
better
Not for us it said in a letter.

So here it ends
The last day for me
And my work friends!

Some have not stayed
New beds they have made.

The doors lock one last time
I came here in my prime
To close it is a crime.

Now old and grey
For all my colleagues
I wish luck
I hope they don't get truly stuck.

Weather Report

Come to the British Isles!
We have a pastime in which all
exaggerate.
Conversations from gate to gate!
This favourite pastime is when
we do unite;
It's all very civil and extremely
polite.

We talk about the weather,
Different every day!
From Land's End to John o'Groats
It really floats our boats!
From cities to places quite remote.

Is that a spot of rain?
Get home or get soaked to the
bone,
In this we must not roam!

That's raining cats and dogs.
Good weather for the ducks,
Good for the spawning frogs!
Not great for all the muddy dogs!

Still it's good for the garden,
Oh look, it's gone to seed, that
will be The blimmin' weeds!

Look at the hail!
Stones as big as your head,
That's exaggerating,
They might smash the garden
shed!

It's lashing down,
Here comes the thunder.
I hope the flash don't strike those
trees.
Oh no, the garden's all covered in
leaves!

Oh look, the sun's shining
through the rain.
Is that a rainbow over there?
Those colours are bright, oh what
a beautiful sight.

Coo! The sun's so sticky!
It's a drier heat abroad!
I am sweating buckets!
I can't flippin' breathe!

Apparently it is hotter than the
Med,
So the man on the telly said!
Oh no, the sun's burnt me head!

It's not as chilly as it looks!
The frost was sharp,
It was very thick.
I saw the gritting lorry.
Mind you don't slip,
You'll put out your hip.

The heating is going on,
Sorry for the soaring bill,
Look at the ice on the window sill.

My goodness, look at that snow!
That caught us on the hop!
Let's get to the shop, before they
run out,
We might not be able to get
about!

That was worse in 47, when the
snow was proper.
Careful: you might come a
cropper!

We used to dig our way out!
Give us a shout if you can't get
about.

That wasn't much
It's been washed away,
That's a shame, it wasn't here to
stay.

So if you are anywhere in this
United
Kingdom
Expect a report from local experts,
About what's coming from above
as it's perceived,
From this conversation you won't
be reprieved.

Artists Need an Audience

The brush that strokes the canvas
The pen that writes the book
The ear that listens to a tune
The eyes that watch the play
unfold
The machine that sews the cloth
The hands that shape the pot
The chisel that carves the wood
The feet that tread the boards
The toes that dance the ballet
The voice that shatters glasses

These are artists' traits
Artists need an audience
To see and touch the things they
create.

Artists need an audience
To criticise and like things they make.
This is missing in the present state of mind
Artists need an audience
To help them unwind.

Where is the audience?
Where did they go?

All the creations waiting to be seen
Waiting to be heard
Waiting to be touched!

All the work is waiting
The eyes are not viewing
No plays renewing
The ears not listening
No tears glistening!

The clapping hands are silent
All the seats are empty
Mind spaces wanting to be filled
Feelings to be embraced
Songs being written
For which we may be smitten!

Artists need an audience!

Something's swept the land
They are all at home.

Technology found a different way
All the people will now have their
say
The creations come into the light of
day
The artist has a new audience.

A gallery that's virtual for hungry
eyes!
Join us zooming to sing our songs
A multi verse of faces in roomy
places
From afar and near
Steering stories as they unfold
On screen they are told.

Sit and watch someone create
Which you can relate
This will release endorphins in your
present mind state

Artists need an audience!

Audiences become a show of faces
As they have had to vacate the
places.

Artists need an audience!

They are all still here
Just not in person
See the online show
The audience never did go
They have been waiting to see
Shows
Creations!

Artists need an audience!

As they all emerge
The world will be more enriched
In the creations they have shared
So now they are in a better place
To look and listen and appreciate.

Artists need an audience
More now than before
To be adored more!

41

Forty-Two

Now Mr Adams, you said it was
the answer!
In this thing of which you write
Let me tell you something that
should make us all take note.

Life is unique in each and
everything!
Never is the same the path that we
follow!
Some play a long game
We cannot blame people for lives
that they lead
It's the life they are born into with
which they proceed.

To say the answer is forty-two
Is quite well hollow
For lives we lead are not that
shallow
For this I do not follow!

As for the universe that goes onto
no end.
To the number forty-two it will not
bend.
Its time
Its size
Is bigger than minds can perceive
So this information
Well it's hard to receive!

Infinitely big
Infinitely small
There is no limit
Really not at all!

We hardly have the answers
What's it all about?
Our insignificance is in no doubt!

Forty-two for everything
A thing no one could know
No one knows everything
It really would show!

I know it was fiction
Very good it was
The fish that translates I can relate
Oh, and that fancy restaurant at
the end of time
Also the tip with the towel for inter
dimensional travel was a valued
point.

So Mr Adams, if smiling from
above
Without a pointed frown
Don't Panic!
It took me 42 minutes to get it all
down!

I Sketched a Man

I sketched a man!
His lines of life mapped a face of
years
One that had laughed
And shed many tears.

Looking from eyes that still
gleamed
Corners with lines of laughter.

Glowing with the soul of satire
Sometimes retired in depths of
sleep
With dreams, so deep.

Framed by eyebrows, bushy
Like flecks of wire
Up to lines of deepened frowns
To receding hair that once hung
down
To shade the eyes
Now in patches around the ears
Not holding back his years.

The rounded blushing whisky nose
Moves down to the pursed chapped
lips
With a bluish tint they take a hint
at the
Words of wisdom
Anger
Jokes all spoke!

When his spirit is awoken
In haze to get through the days

Beneath his squared but ageing
chin
There is a dimple
It makes him look wise
Complex
Not simple!

Today I sketched a man
With each pencil line
Brush strokes of colour
The tones of his life
The character there within
Appeared on the canvas mask
To capture was quite a task.

I Sketched a Woman

Today I sketched a woman.

Her eyes sparkling with a sea of blue
Giving out hope
In a piercing confident gaze
Putting onlookers into a haze.

Her eyebrows in strict lines
With pencil strokes these defined.

Her hair shined a false red
Although authority it defined
Not ever to be undermined.

Her shoulders the artificial red
cascaded
In locks so fine
Ears lost, face outlined.

Her button nose
Met ruby lips, dimples at each end
Embedded in blushing cheeks
Knowledge this face did seek.

Today I sketched a woman.

Strong in demeanour
Beneath this world of knowledge
Looked out the girl from the
Woman she had become.
I hope the sketch
Portrayed the layers of beauty
After all this was my duty.

Trees Know

Once they were seeds upon the
wind!
Falling across the land
Casting roots to make foundations.
The shoots of growth drank in the
rain
The wise old forests they became.

More seeds were carried by
wildlife
This helped them populate.
In the world they grew tall from
things so small.

They grew blissful of the world
around
As they became many
They gave the world the lungs to
breathe
This gift was well received.

Animals made homes and became
Reliant on the peaceful rustling
giants.

Then came humans, chop, cut, saw
For this destruction they had not
foresaw.

The world began to suffocate
As the guardians became less and
less
The lands became distressed.

Build, build
Choke, choke
Here comes the belching smoke
To supply the urban forests

The trees knew this would cause
despair
The world would need repair
So the men became aware.

If they didn't stop and take stock
Seas would rise
Lands would demise
Become no more.

So mankind must strive
Make the world a better place!
Walk with nature into a clearer
future!

So the trees whisper on the wind
Make the world much cleaner
It then will become greener.

So listen to nature's plea
Use the resources in moderation
Don't destroy it with modernisation!

Trees know!

Where Are All The People?

The land became deserted!
Quiet as a mouse!
They had all retreated from
house to house

The frog jumped up and said,
"Where are all the people?
Prodding round my pond?"
"Yes," hissed the fox,
"Where did they abscond?"

"No litter on the ground,"
The owl hooted past.
"Not a sound or a bottle
discarded on the grass."

"Where's the sound of a horn?
Or the cars on the road?"
Ribbited the toad.

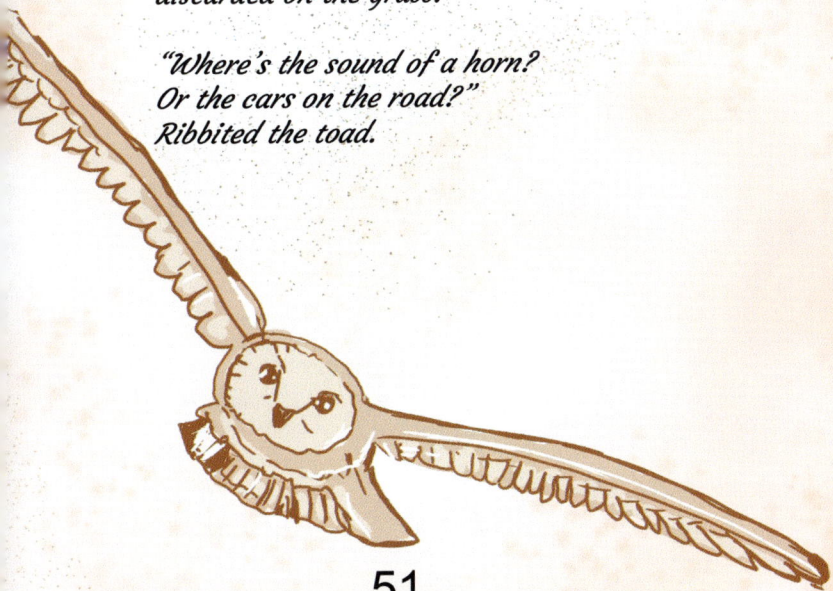

51

The little bird tweeted,
"They are all inside,
I have seen some walking in the
countryside."

"The air I can now breathe,
It's hard to perceive that the
pollution has gone that they
usually do leave,"
Squawked the crows,
Swirling round in the air.

"Let's see if we can see in the
towns what's dragged them all
down, all down?"
Said a deer, the animals he did
steer.

The animals wandered in and out
Looking to see who was about.
They were all in doubt when the
People began to shout inside their
dens,
Startling a group of nosey old
hens.

53

"There are people all queuing not
like before. I wonder what for?"
Said the circling kestrel,
In the sky he did soar.

Then they returned, but not the
same as before.
The world they seemed to now
defend.
The world became more
understanding, a message they
did send.
It was truly on the mend.

The animals did wonder what
took place that year,
It really was not clear.
Now all the people they did no
longer fear!

Virtual World

Are we living virtually?
I haven't seen my friends, you see
They've zoomed and skyped online
Spending some time to convey a
message
From far away or close by
Is it here to stay?

Faces resembling sheets of stamps
These little mouths, chat, chat
Talking of this and that.

A birthday we all toast
Or play along to an online quiz
Some sing to entertain
Others dance around a room.

Are we real any more?
I am not sure
So I go out the door
Yes it's all still in place!

They locked it down
Around the world!

We could not see or do the things
we always do
As the world does recover I'm not
sure what's virtual or real anymore!

As people distance to deliver post
We peer through masks of hope
We stand apart to come together
The world will be real again.

What's real?
What's normal?
Do we know?
Let's show the world which way to
go.
What's right?
What's wrong?
Make a real not virtual future
A world in which we can all
venture.

Sea of Faces

Today I went by train to a busy
place
Here I saw face after face!
All types and every sort
Some were in deep thought.
Like a wave they washed over
streets.

Some were neat
Some unwashed
Some laughed
Some cried
Some frowned
Some looked a little down

All moved together like a tide
All were trying to get to a
destination.

So come on, step aside
Each focused on their own goal
Like some massive shoal.

Thieves looking for the next job
Looking to see who they can rob.
Others looking at sale prices
Some ready to indulge in their own
vices.

So then the tide went out
No faces upon the streets
No feet moving to a rhythmic beat
In their houses they did stay
Waiting for the day the tide would
return.

For a while in their homes they did
sit
Where the faces sit and talk
Ponder on a long walk
Thinking of the life they may lead.

One day caught up in the tide
Into the sea of faces they will slide.

Another Day

The sunrise shines out for another
day.
What path will it take?
Will it be a make or break?
The kind of day changing
Weaving in every way!

Where will it go?
To what destination will it lead?
Is it likely to impede what we do?
Or previous days decisions undo?
Then we will concede
So no further it may lead!

Today may make us happy
Or we might be sad.
Emotions through the day may be
invoked!
Words of wisdom may be spoken
Comfort could be awoken!
Or a joke may be told
To the laughter we are sold.

We may plan for other days
Maybe book our holidays!
Or days of work for a business
meet
Maybe for a party in the street!
Make plans ahead of time
Or own the day, made yours.

It may be the start of a new career
Perhaps diploma to set for the
future
Today maybe I will meet my spouse
Or plan to buy a house.
Maybe friendships will be made
Old ones made more solid
Or from words spoken
They will be broken.

Was it just another day?
Never waste them they do say
Eventually it will be your final day
Then there won't be another day.

Humour

Humour can be a funny old thing
It can make you sing out loud
Sing a little ditty that's quite witty.

You may laugh so much, you may
cry
Some of it can be very dry.

Cackling folk telling drawn out
tales
With an end which ensues
collective laughs.

Some will get it
Some will not
Some heads it will go over
Like a fleeting bird
Don't get what you said
It's quite absurd

It can be well timed
Others they will mime
It must be delivered with panache
Punchline still intact.

Sometimes from a frowning clown
Will lift you up when you are down.
So lift up that upside-down smile
You will walk a happy mile.

Some jokes will offend
Others will have no end
It could be in a meme
Who knows, maybe a viral gem?

If it can make you see the funny
side
Then laugh out loud
Put your worries to one side
Life, it's a funny old ride.

So to go through it smiling you can
glide
Until the end you do slide
Happy vibes on your side
Smiles all round your bedside.

Your legacy
They will say you died laughing
You saw the funny side
A frown you could not abide.

63

Tides

Into the world we are all born
Different beliefs across each land
Into the world we now stand.

Thoughts come in waves
From dreams
From moods
Or things we are taught
Some we need to sort.
To move forward in our field
Decide things to which we will
yield.

We are taught about places we
may never visit or see.
So we form opinions from afar
Sometimes social media is our
guiding star.

Listen to the people is what
sometimes we do,
We sometimes imagine what it's
like to walk in their shoes.
This helps decide what we should
do.

So the tides of life wash over us
throughout the years,
It's up to us which direction our
ship we do steer
Maybe towards a life-changing
career,
Or even someone we may endear.

The tides they continue with
seeds that we sow,
Which could decide the directions
on which we may go.

Friendships will be made, solid
they will be.
On many things we will all agree
Don't ever let your friendships be
washed out to sea!

When it's the day of the final
tide
We will ask the question
Was it a life well spent?

I hope you had good health,
A wealth of family,
Good friends,
You succeeded,
Great times you did spend.

I hope I have conveyed good
words to you all,
I have had a great ball.
So I continue my journey on
The Tide of Life,
If you loved this I will be back to
have another crack!

Thanks to all my friends who inspired me and helped me realise this book.